Maria Csernoch
Piroska Biró

Sprego Programming

Maria Csernoch
Piroska Biró

Sprego Programming

LAP LAMBERT Academic Publishing

Impressum / Imprint

Bibliografische Information der Deutschen Nationalbibliothek: Die Deutsche Nationalbibliothek verzeichnet diese Publikation in der Deutschen Nationalbibliografie; detaillierte bibliografische Daten sind im Internet über http://dnb.d-nb.de abrufbar.
Alle in diesem Buch genannten Marken und Produktnamen unterliegen warenzeichen-, marken- oder patentrechtlichem Schutz bzw. sind Warenzeichen oder eingetragene Warenzeichen der jeweiligen Inhaber. Die Wiedergabe von Marken, Produktnamen, Gebrauchsnamen, Handelsnamen, Warenbezeichnungen u.s.w. in diesem Werk berechtigt auch ohne besondere Kennzeichnung nicht zu der Annahme, dass solche Namen im Sinne der Warenzeichen- und Markenschutzgesetzgebung als frei zu betrachten wären und daher von jedermann benutzt werden dürften.

Bibliographic information published by the Deutsche Nationalbibliothek: The Deutsche Nationalbibliothek lists this publication in the Deutsche Nationalbibliografie; detailed bibliographic data are available in the Internet at http://dnb.d-nb.de.
Any brand names and product names mentioned in this book are subject to trademark, brand or patent protection and are trademarks or registered trademarks of their respective holders. The use of brand names, product names, common names, trade names, product descriptions etc. even without a particular marking in this work is in no way to be construed to mean that such names may be regarded as unrestricted in respect of trademark and brand protection legislation and could thus be used by anyone.

Coverbild / Cover image: www.ingimage.com

Verlag / Publisher:
LAP LAMBERT Academic Publishing
ist ein Imprint der / is a trademark of
OmniScriptum GmbH & Co. KG
Heinrich-Böcking-Str. 6-8, 66121 Saarbrücken, Deutschland / Germany
Email: info@lap-publishing.com

Herstellung: siehe letzte Seite /
Printed at: see last page
ISBN: 978-3-659-51689-4

Sprego programming

Abstract

Spreadsheet management is a border-land between office applications and programming, however, it is rather communicated that spreadsheet is nothing more than an easily handled fun piece. Consequently, the complexity of spreadsheet handling, the unprepared end-users, their problem solving abilities and approaches do not match. To overcome these problems we have developed and introduced Sprego (Spreadsheet Lego). Sprego is a simplified functional programming language in spreadsheet environment, and such as can be used both as introductory language and the language of end-user programmers. The essence of Sprego is that we use as few and simple functions as possible and based on these functions build multilevel formulas. With this approach, similar to high level programming, we are able solve advanced problems, developing algorithmic skills, computational thinking. The advantage of Sprego is the simplicity of the language, when the emphasis is not on the coding but on the problem. Beyond that spreadsheets would provide real life problems with authentic data and tables which students are more interested in than the artificial environment and semi-authentic problems of high level programming languages.

Table of Contents

1. Introduction

With the widespread use of computers, we are faced with an increasing number of end-users of birotical (computer-related office tools) software [5], [6], [41], [51], [56], [64], [69], [79]. We have introduced the French based expression "birotical" to clearly distinguish office applications from other computer applications. Applying this expression there is no need for further explanation that which kind of application is meant. Birotical software and documents cover mainly text and spreadsheet management and the resulting documents of these activities.

However, with the high number of untrained and ill-trained end-users an increase in the number of error-prone documents is reported, due to the misuse of birotical software. In the last decade not only rumours of this undesirable and very unfortunate situation have been circulating, researches have proved that the problem does indeed exist [4], [5], [32], [33], [34], [64], [66], [67], [68], [69], [75], [77], [78], [79] and is deeply rooted in the end-users' lack of computational thinking [33], [9], [85]. Their ignorance prevents them evaluating their problem solving skills, their sequences of computer related activities, so the output of these activities [50].

Apart from a very few authors [4], [5], [25], [26], [27], [36], [76], research mainly focuses on spreadsheet documents, and the consequences of spreadsheet errors. However, we have to note here that the main reason that spreadsheets receive more attention than other birotical documents is because of the financial consequences. While not-properly handled text-based documents mainly cause isolated cases of misunderstanding, miscomprehension, and misinterpretation, until spreadsheets play fundamental roles in the financial world.

1.1. Sources of misinterpretation

The question, in general, is what has led us to this situation, and what would be the solutions to reduce the number of errors in these documents. This is a fundamental question for education. It has been realized that despite the attempts to introduce formal Computer Sciences/Informatics education, and rearrange classical school

3

subjects by considering digital competency in primary and secondary education, the students' level of computational thinking has not met our expectations [7], [8], [11], [12], [34], [35]. According to the most extreme opinions, birotical software is to blame [44], [45]; however, this is not justified. Programs themselves are harmless, they work on algorithms; the problem arises when teaching does not focus on the algorithm-driven feature of programs. Teachers are responsible for giving proper instructions which would lead to the development of the students' digital literacy, algorithmic skills, computational thinking [40], [21], [49], [85].

Teacher education, however, has to deal with a triad of circumstances: the human-computer interaction, the novelty of this school subject, as well as the commercialized world that has developed around it. The basis of the problems arises from the communication between humans and "dump" computers. To reach a high level of communication between humans and computers we have to develop computational thinking of humans, and to achieve this formal education is needed. However, for formal education, teachers are needed, and for teachers, teacher-education is needed. At this point the loop is closed, and we are faced with the chicken and the egg problem: who teaches the teachers if there are no teachers? The lack of proper teacher education led us to a situation in which teachers were looking for help and for solutions. The software companies were ready to answer with their commercial-based software. Their emphasis is on user-friendly interfaces, bombarding both teachers and end-users with ever newer features, without any scientifically proven appropriacy.

These circumstances lead end-users to bricolage [4], [5], the unplanned usage of GUI (Graphical User Interface), the superiority of surface approach problem solving TAEW-based methods (Trial-and-Error Wizard-based) [33], [9], and consequently, to the thousands of error-prone documents.

The students' do not see the algorithms behind computer problem solving, and they accept computer tools, both hardware and software, unconditionally. Testing university students of Informatics (TAaAS project, Testing Algorithmic and

4

Application Skills, [7]–[12], [31]–[35]) we found several indicators to this approach, which is well represented in their remarks.

Figure 1: Students' answers to "What happens when you double click on a document file?"

In the self-evaluation session of the same project (TAaAS), we asked the students to list 15 spreadsheet functions which they think the most important. All together the survey resulted in 99 most important functions, and the most extreme answer is presented in Figure 2. Finding the reasons for this incredibly high number of functions mentioned by the students, we checked the coursebooks available in Hungary. What would be your guess? (In the Hungarian spreadsheet coursebooks one-hundred and seventy-two functions are mentioned) The result explains a lot. These sources are rather users' guides, repeating the helps, and do not match the requirements of coursebooks, actually they are false teaching materials.

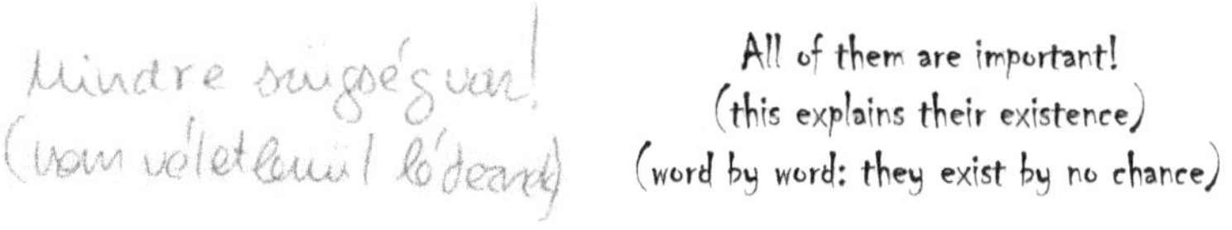

Figure 2: Student thinks that all the functions of spreadsheets are important (the original message (left) and its translation (right))

We can conclude that surface approach methods should not have this overwhelming power. However, methods can be developed which would change, first of all the teachers', and then the end-users' attitude towards computers, and birotical software, so that ultimately, students would achieve well-developed computational thinking and algorithmic skills. We have no other task but to abandon TAEW-based problem solving methods, and replace them with deep-approach metacognitive methods. The theoretical background (Section 3), the details and the characteristics of CAAD-based (Computer Algorithmic and Debugging) methods are presented in the consecutive section (Section4), and further examples in Sprego at the end of the article (Section 8).

5

In the following two subsections of Introduction we provide a fast overview of the method entitled Sprego. In Chapter 2 the main research questions and hypotheses are presented. Chapter 3 provides the detailed theoretical background of this novel method. In Chapter 4 the details of Sprego is provided with examples and with additional examples in Chapter 8. It is your choice in which order you read these sections. You can keep their sequential order, but you also have the option starting with Chapter 4 and 8, focusing on programming in Sprego, and turn back later on to the theoretical background.

1.2. Sprego

Within the frame of spreadsheets we invented a method entitled Sprego programming, Sprego for short. The title of the method is the abbreviation of Spreadsheet Lego.

The main idea of Sprego is that we handle spreadsheets as an introductory programming language for novice and end-user programmers. In this sense, we use the operators of the spreadsheet language and as few and as simple general-purpose functions as possible, and based on these simple tools we built multilevel functions and formulas. With our deep-approach problem solving method (Section 3.2) [22], [38], [55], [7], [10], [33] we are able to solve computer related problems with an approach which is well-accepted in other programming paradigms: detecting the problem, building algorithms, coding, debugging.

In a spreadsheet environment the main activity is data retrieval. In Sprego we can take advantage both of the environment and the functional language; the data retrieval will be carried out with methods adapted from other programming languages.

In spite of the theoretical background which has been available for several years, a complete system with a methodology for teaching has not emerged.

Within the frame of the TAaAS project, we have been testing Sprego in the last four years. In the testing process, we run three tests: a pre-test, before starting Sprego, a post-test, after covering Sprego, and a delayed post-test, one year later. The change in the students' results proves the effectiveness of the method. Without any details, the figures are the following: 5–10%, 60–70%, and 40–50%, in the pre-, post-, and delayed post-tests, respectively [9], [28], [33]. In the opinion of the pre-service teachers of Informatics, Sprego has the following characteristics [37]):

- Creating multilevel formulas helps to develop algorithmic skills.
- Using Sprego requires thinking.
- Sprego helps developing logical thinking.
- The characteristics of the simple, general purpose functions are easier to see [than those of the problem specific functions].
- Sprego gives spreadsheet knowledge for later [post-school] usage.
- The more conscious usage of arguments.
- The general purpose functions can be used in wider context.
- Instead of HLOOKUP() and VLOOKUP(), the use of the INDEX(MATCH()) multilevel function is much more interesting, since it requires more thinking.

1.3. The samples used in the paper

We would like to emphasize that the tables and samples presented in this paper do not follow the order of their introduction to classes. They rather serve to demonstrate the joint power which the simple general purpose functions with multilevel functions together carry within themselves.

However, the sample tables clearly demonstrate one further advantage of Sprego programming. If we use authentic tables with which students can do real data retrieval, they will not find the program useless and superficial – in LOGO, [61] and in high level programming languages, respectively –, as is typical when students are not really motivated and enthusiastic about programming.

7

2. Hypotheses

H1. Sprego fulfils the requirements of the deep-approach metacognitive methods; consequently, it can be used for teaching programming and end-user programming.

H2. Array formulas support Sprego programming, and serve problem solving better than the built-in functions.

H3. Sprego eliminates the commercialized side effects of spreadsheet languages.

H4. Sprego supports compatibility between different spreadsheet programs and different versions.

H5. Sprego is less error-prone than traditional spreadsheet tools and approaches.

3. Theoretical background

The first suggestions for using spreadsheet as an introductory programming language date back to the late 80s (in [62]), and early 90s [62], and have been raised several times [63], [83], [71], but a complete system with a teaching methodology for proper use has not yet been created.

3.1. Should we teach students to program?

There are opinions which state that not everyone should learn programming. However, Soloway, along with his fellow educators [74], and later on Ben-Ari [6] stated that programming and algorithmic skills – to use the recently developed expression – computational thinking [85], should be taught and can be taught to everyone, only the environment should be matched to the requirements of the students. It is not necessarily the demanding high level programming languages which would be the only solution, and especially not as a first language - there are several other possibilities available [72], [63], [65], [83], [71], [80], [6]. We share this latter idea, and based on it, we have developed our method to support Sprego. Coding is not something superficial, but is a method which is necessary in order to

8

communicate effectively with computers; beyond this, there is a wide range of sources to develop the skills which are required to carry out this communication.

3.2. Deep and surface metacognitive problem solving approaches

The different metacognitive problem solving methods were categorized by Case et al [17], [18], [19], [20] as deep and surface approach methods. The deep surface approach is further specialized as a conceptual-based approach, while two further groups of the surface approach methods are defined: algorithmic and information based. We have realized, however, that these groups of problem solving methods do not cover recently emerged computer related activities. Considering all these, two further groups, one deep and one surface approach, were added to the already well accepted system.

The computer connected deep approach category, known as Computer Algorithmic and Debugging (CAAD) based [33], covers those sequences of activities which are required to carry out algorithm-driven programming tasks, from the analysis of the problem to the close of the process by checking the correctness of the activities carried out [33].

To the original surface approach categories the Trial-and-Error Wizard based methods are added [33]. They are those computer-specialized activities which gained have strength with the spread of the GUI, and are highly supported by software companies. This approach claims that to carry out computer related activities there is no need for algorithms, since the GUI support is enough to produce the output. The problem with this method is that its focus is not on real problem solving but on reaching an end result. The two phenomena and the methods based on them are not identical.

We have to note here that in 1992 Booth [13] found four different approaches to program writing; two deep and two surface approach groups, but her results have remained isolated. Comparing our system, which is the expansion of Case et al's, to

Booth's findings, we can draw the following conclusions (C&G, B, Cs&B refer to publications by Case and Gunstone, Booth, Csernoch and Biró, respectively):

–   conceptual (C&G) → structural (B)
–   CAAD (Cs&B) → operational (B)
–   algorithmic (C&G) → expedient (B)
–   information (C&G) → constructional (B)
–   TAEW (Cs&B) → GUI navigation

Our purpose with Sprego is to introduce a deep approach metacognitive method, with which the students' algorithmic skills can be effectively and efficiently developed.

3.3. Minimalist theory

We have to keep in mind that in our concept spreadsheet languages would serve as an introductory language for beginners, and a suitable language for those who do not want to be professional programmers, but well-skilled end-users. Considering this point of view, spreadsheet languages and approaches such as Sprego should be taught with a minimalist approach [16], [63], [54], and consequently, the methods developed for teaching high level programming languages for novices can be applied to this language.

The process of programming is exactly the same as we are familiar with from high level programming languages (See Sections 4.3, 4.4, and 8). The advantages of spreadsheet languages in general, compared to high level programming languages, are that the coding is less demanding, there is no need for explicit declarations, and the phenomena of function is familiar from studies in Mathematics. A further simplification of the language, compared to high level programming languages, is that in the spreadsheet environment we do not write, but just call already existing functions. One further step would be, as suggested by several researchers, to write functions [2], [65], but this is not our intention at present.

However, we have seen from the reported error-prone spreadsheet documents that all these advantages do not guarantee an algorithmic approach to spreadsheet problems

10

[3], [52], [53]. We have found in our previous research that all of these advantages would be diminished with the TAEW-based approach to spreadsheet [9], [28], [29], [30], [31], [32], [33]; the endless new features, the high number of functions (Sections 4.3.2 and 4.3.3), the demanding and large number of arguments (Section 4.4), the unplanned wondering and rummaging around in the GUI.

Sprego focuses, on one hand, on the further simplification of the language, by using as few functions as possible (for the list of Sprego functions see Table 1); on the other hand, it focuses on the generalization of the language, by using general purpose functions. With these tools multilevel functions can be built and a wider range of problems can be solved than with the problem-specific functions of spreadsheet programs (for details see Sections 4.3.2, 4.3.3, and 4.4). Frequent use and coding with a few simple general functions would result in users remembering them and working with them in an error-free way.

Since the coding in spreadsheets is not demanding, the typing of the codes is highly recommended. We have to keep in mind the fact that the coding also should follow the minimalist approach, and as is detailed in Section 4.2, it should start with the more internal functions, when the formula is the simplest, and should be developed step by step in an outwards direction [15], [24]. A further simplification of coding in Sprego is the usage of array formulas (for details see Sections 4.3, 4.4, and 8). These tools would prepare students for handling arrays, creating and debugging source codes in high level programming languages.

As in other programming languages, at the beginning the minimalist approach should be accompanied with full guidance, especially in case of non-programmers, which would help the students to develop their algorithmic skills [14], [54], [57], [60], [70].

We can conclude that with the minimalist approach supporting Sprego, the focus is not on the language, but on the problems, which is one of the key issues in teaching programming [13]. This allows students to focus on the problem, since the language is not a barrier; it only plays a marginal role.

3.4. Spreadsheet language

Spreadsheets are visual, first-order functional languages [65], and considering the number of users, they are the most popular programming systems in use today [1]. As has been proved, functional languages would serve effectively as first languages [13], being more reliable than imperative languages, using the familiar phenomenon of the function, letting the user focus more on the problem than on the coding, and consequently, producing fewer errors [1], [13].

However, the high number of spreadsheet documents containing errors does not seem to be in accordance with the high expectations of the more traditional functional languages. As has already been mentioned in Sections 1.1 and 3.3, and proved in our previously published works, this is mainly due to the TAEW-based problem solving methods, which are highly favoured and supported by the GUI. However, we cannot neglect the fact that the number of end-users makes the relevance of spreadsheet among functional languages even greater [1]. Previous attempts to improve spreadsheet languages have mainly focused on its approximation to traditional programming languages.

Sprego focuses on the already available tools of spreadsheet languages in harmony with the features of traditional functional languages.

- Spreadsheet programs perform automatic recalculation: whenever the contents of a cell have been edited, all cells that are directly or transitively dependent on that cell are recalculated [71].
- Spreadsheet programs distinguish between several types of data, such as numbers, text strings, logical values (Booleans), and arrays. However, this distinction is made dynamically [71].
- Functional languages have a very small syntax and a logically well-defined semantics [13].
- Functional languages are more problem-oriented than conventional languages [43].

12

- Functional languages have a simple mathematical basis, the lambda calculus, and because of the lack of side-effects, program correctness proofs are easier [43].
- The intuitive understanding of functions that the students bring with them from their school mathematics studies, should be an advantage when studying a functional programming language which exploits this before they study the imperative languages [13]. Based on this theoretical background, we understand function in a semantic sense, as a mapping rather than any sort of syntax ("code") for the function [42].

3.5. Levels of mastery

Beyond the already mentioned disadvantages of the TAEW-based methods, one of the main weaknesses of the method is that it does not follow the recommended order of levels of mastery [21]. The major characteristic of the TAEW-based methods is that the first level, the understanding the concept, is skipped over, and the second level, the usage is taken as the starting level. This is what Gove [44], [45] mixed up when he was discussing teaching Word and Excel, instead of text and spreadsheet management. The consequences of leaving out the first level of mastery are aimless clicking and error-prone documents. Consequently, there is no chance to reach the third level of mastery, where students would be able to consider a concept from multiple viewpoints and/or justify the selection of a particular approach to solve a problem [21].

4. Results – Sprego

Considering the theoretical background we had to find out whether the tools to build Sprego and its teaching methodology were available in the spreadsheet languages. Three tools were required, and regardless of the programs and their versions, they are all available.

Spreadsheet tools for Sprego:

- Simple, general-purpose language blocks: using as few and as simple functions as possible (Sprego functions, Section 4.1, Table 1).
- The ability to define new structures: creating multilevel functions and formulas (Section 4.2).
- Array formulas: eliminating the copying of formulas (Section 4.3).
- Debugging: The combination of the Sprego functions with the multilevel array formulas makes thorough debugging available in spreadsheets. Similar to high level programming languages, both manual and spreadsheet supported debugging can be carried out (Section 4.4).
- Authentic sources: By using authentic tables in the teaching of Sprego we would avoid the fiasco of other school programming languages. Most of the students find the programming languages designed for educational purposes useless. They are not able to transfer knowledge from the school programs to solve real word problems in other environments. With Sprego we can provide the students with real world problems; consequently, there is no gap between the student and the end user statuses (Figures 4, 6, and 7).

By applying these tools we are able to solve spreadsheet problems of differing complexity, without the desire for ever newer amendments to the spreadsheet programs, the endless searching for problem- and program-specific built-in functions, and endless rummaging around in the helps and supports. Consequently, in Sprego the emphasis is not on the language and on the GUI, but on the problems, which would serve at least two purposes: providing an introductory language for professional programmers [13] and a language for end-user programmers [62], [63], [83].

4.1. Sprego functions

For beginners, fewer than ten simple, general-purpose functions would serve as a starting kit to write programs in spreadsheets (Table 1, Sprego1). As students advance in spreadsheet programming the need for a few more functions would arise. However, we have to keep in mind that general-purpose functions should be introduced, not those which are invented for solving special problems. Considering these principles, moving from the functions introduced from the very beginning to those introduced as we advance towards professionalism, we can group them into three sets. The dozen functions of Sprego1 and Sprego2 are compulsory for everyone (Sprego12), even for novices. Sprego3 is optional, and additional simple functions would be added to this group, depending on the development and interest of the students [9], [29], [37].

In addition to the already mentioned advantages of using and building our own formulas, there is one more which should be mentioned here; there is a great probability that new problems will arise for which there is no built-in function (Task 5 and Task 9).

Table 1: The introduction of spreadsheet functions for novice end-user programmers, starting with group Sprego1, adding the functions of Sprego2 later on, while Sprego3 is optional

Sprego1	Sprego2	Sprego3
SUM()	MATCH()	SMALL()
AVERAGE()	INDEX()	LARGE()
MIN()	ISERROR()	AND()
MAX()		OR()
LEFT()		NOT()
RIGHT()		ROW()
LEN()		COLUMN()
SEARCH()		OFFSET()
IF()		SUBSTITUTE()
		TRANSPOSE()
		ROUND()
		RAND()
		INT()

To match the requirements of other programming languages the IF() function has to be included in group Sprego1. However, we have to note here that the official descriptions of the IF() function have to be reworded, because end-users, especially

15

novices, do not understand them. The reason is simple: they just do not have the vocabulary and the background knowledge to understand *condition*, *test*, *logical test* [48]. The following list is a selection of descriptions of IF() function from spreadsheet wizards and helps which untrained end-users and students do not understand.

- "logical test: The condition that you want to check" [23].
- "test is or refers to a logical value or expression that returns a logical value (TRUE or FALSE)" [46].
- "Test is any value or expression that can be TRUE or FALSE" [47].

Table 2: The reworded description of the IF() function

argument	the role of the argument
1.	yes/no question
2.	the output of the function if the answer to the question is yes
3.	the output of the function if the answer to the question is no
IF(yes/no_question,output_if_the_answer_is_yes,output_if_the_answer_is_no)	

Sprego programming focuses heavily on the usage of variables. The method is borrowed from the traditional programming languages to make the programs/documents less error-prone. In spreadsheet management there are two options for variables: we can use the default names of the cells and arrays with the spreadsheet references or we can give custom names.

4.2. Creating multilevel formulas

The other tool for solving problems in this minimalist spreadsheet environment is the ability to create multilevel functions. Depending on the age group to which Sprego programming is introduced,

- the phenomenon of function and multilevel function would be familiar, and with Sprego word problem solving based on authentic data would be learnt,
- Sprego programming can be used to introduce the phenomenon,
- it is an environment enabling us to practice how values would be transferred from the internal function to the external function, and to understand the

16

relation between the domain and range of the functions in this hyponym and hypernym relationship.

In this approach to spreadsheet management students understand that functions in a formula can be embedded into each other. The output of the innermost function is the argument of the function around it; its output value is the argument of the next function around it, and so on, until we reach the outermost function, whose output is the output of the whole multilevel formula. The functions hold each other just like the popular matryoshka dolls do (Figure 3).

Figure 3: The structure of multilevel functions is similar to that of the matryoshka dolls [87]

The realization of the multilevel functions should follow the evaluation order. This means that first the innermost functions should be constructed and evaluated. If this is done correctly, we can expand the formula and the results appear in the same array (Table 14 and Table 15). Here we create the function outside to the first one, using its output value as an argument of the outside function.

4.3. Array formulas

There are several possible tools in spreadsheet management which support deep-approach metacognitive problem solving. In the following, array formulas (AF) are introduced, one of the possible solutions. Array formulas are a long-existing feature of spreadsheets, but somehow they have never reached the status they deserve; the introduction of array handling without the complexity known in high level programming languages [81], [82], [84], [30], [71], [80], [86].

In general, we distinguish between two different kinds of array formulas and their combinations.

– The output by default is an array.

17

- The output by default is one value, but the default non-array argument(s) are substituted by an array(s).

- The combination of the types above, when both arguments and output values are non-default arrays.

There is one further group of array formulas which are worth mentioning: conditional array formulas. This group of formulas would fit into any of the three groups listed above; however, its significance from several different points of view gives it a special status. The great advantage of conditional array formulas is that they are able to substitute built-in problem-specific functions. Functions designed to solve special problems are highly program- and version dependent, and one of the barricades to an effective use of spreadsheet programs [9], [10], [28], [29], [30], [31], [32], [33], [37].

	A	B	C	D	F	G
1	State	Abbr.	Capital	Largest city	Population	Total area in mi2 (km2)
2	Alabama	AL	Montgomery	Birmingham	4833722	700452420000000000052,420 (135,767)
3	Alaska	AK	Juneau	Anchorage	735132	700566538400000000665,384 (1,723,337)
4	Arizona	AZ	Phoenix	Phoenix	6626624	700511399000000000113,990 (295,233)
5	Arkansas	AR	Little Rock	Little Rock	2959373	700453179000000000053,179 (137,733)
16	Iowa	IA	Des Moines	Des Moines	3090416	700456273000000000056,273 (145,746)
17	Kansas	KS	Topeka	Wichita	2893957	700482278000000000082,278 (213,099)
18	Kentucky[C]	KY	Frankfort	Louisville	4395295	700440408000000000040,408 (104,656)
19	Louisiana	LA	Baton Rouge	New Orleans	4625470	700452378000000000052,378 (135,658)
38	Oregon	OR	Salem	Portland	3930065	700498379000000000098,379 (254,800)
39	Pennsylvania[E]	PA	Harrisburg	Philadelphia	12773801	700446054000000000046,054 (119,279)
40	Rhode Island[F]	RI	Providence	Providence	1051511	700315450000000001,545 (4,002)
41	South Carolina	SC	Columbia	Columbia	4774839	700432020000000000032,020 (82,931)
50	Wisconsin	WI	Madison	Milwaukee	5742713	700465496000000000065,496 (169,634)
51	Wyoming	WY	Cheyenne	Cheyenne	582658	700497813000000000097,813 (253,335)

Figure 4: Table extracted from the List of states and territories of the United States webpage [88]

4.3.1. Multiple-result array formulas

Array output as default

There are functions whose output by default is an array – a vector or a matrix. Two of the most commonly used functions in this group is the pair of the TRANSPOSE() (Formula 3) function and the INDEX() function with a vector output – when one of the index arguments of the function is set to 0 (Formulas 1 or 2).

18

To close and evaluate an array formula not a simple Enter should be used but the Ctrl + Shift + Enter combination in Windows (Excel, Calc), and Cmd + Enter in MacOS. The resulting formula is compassed around with curly braces.

Task 1:   Create a cross-reference table of the names of the states (Figure 4).

The characteristics of Task 1

- In the original table the names of the states are arranged in a vertical vector.
- The vector should be transformed into a horizontal vector.
- The first component of the original vector goes into the second column, which is column B, the second component into the third column, which is column C, and so on. The index of the states in the original vector is one less than their new column.

The algorithm of Task 1

- The names of the states come from the A2:A51 vector.
- The new vector is a horizontal vector, so all the components go into a new column, from left to right.
- The position of the column decreased by 1 gives the index of components of the original vector.
- These two data provides the two arguments of the INDEX() function.

The coding of Task 1

$$\{=\text{INDEX}(A2{:}A51,\text{COLUMN}()-1,0))\} \tag{1}$$

As the name of this group of formulas suggests, the output is an array. To display all the results of the formula the output array has to be defined. The method with which arrays can be defined is one of the advantages of spreadsheet interfaces; there is nothing else to do but select the suitable range on the worksheet. If the array needed is too big for the screen we can make further use of the advantages of the GUI; we can hide rows and columns (for examples see Figure 4, Figure 6, and Figure 7), and we can switch between the two types of reference to the one which is more

19

convenient – for selecting the array the R1C1 (Table 5, left sample), while for creating formulas it is the A1 type which is more convenient (compare Formula 1 to Formula 2). For novice and end-user programmers it is a great advantage of the GUI that there is no need for the definition and declaration of the variables and the arrays in the code.

$$\{=\text{INDEX}(R[1]C[-1]:R[50]C[-1],\text{COLUMN}()-1,0)\} \tag{2}$$

The problem can also be solved with the TRANSPOSE() function from group Sprego3, which is also a general purpose function, but one more function to remember. Consequently, we suggest using the more common the INDEX() function, presented in Formula 1.

$$\{=\text{TRANSPOSE}(A2:A51)\} \tag{3}$$

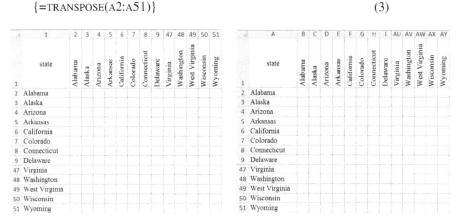

Figure 5: The cross reference table of the states displayed in the R1C1 (left) and the A1 (right) reference types

Array output as non-default

The non-default array output supersedes the copying of formulas, which is an error-prone technique [65], [64]. This characteristic of the multiple-result array formulas is remarkable, since one of the major sources of errors in spreadsheet document is rooted in the copying of formulas.

The non-default multiple-result array formulas are created from function(s), at least one of whose default argument(s) is overruled by an array. Since the result is an array, to display all the output values, the array has to be defined and selected.

The application of array formulas instead of error-prone copying has several advantages:

- There is one formula instead of many.
- There is no need for re-copying when the formula is changed.
- The formula is secured, since none but the first occasion of the formula can be modified, which is in the first cell of the array.

Relying on all of these advantages, building multilevel formulas from the inside outwards is extremely simple. Once we have the algorithm there is nothing else to do but create the formula in the first cell of the array, and select the array for the formula. From this point on, the modifications can be applied to the first occasion, which is the first cell of the array, and then the whole array is filled in with the new values.

In the following examples all the formulas are array formulas, either single or multiple result array formulas. By solving the problems, we always start with the most inside function, and this very same formula is extended and evaluated in each step. The outputs of the consecutive formulas are presented in the evaluation tables connected to each task.

Task 2:   Remove the leading Space from the names of the states (Figure 4, Table 3).

The characteristics of Task 2

- The names of the states have different lengths (D for differences).
- Each name is preceded by one Space (S for similarities).
- The new string is one character shorter than the original (S).
- The string which should be cut out from the original is on the right side (S).

The algorithm of Task 2

-   Deciding the length of the original string (Formula 4),
-   Deciding the length of the shorter string (Formula 5)
-   Cutting out the shorter string from the right side of the original string (Formula 6).

In the following, to solve the given problems sequences of array formulas are created by editing already existing formulas, starting with the first one. The first sequence of formulas is presented in Formulas 4–6). For editing a formula we have to switch to the formula editing bar. To do this we can use the F2 function key or the Control + U key combination in Windows or MacOS, respectively, or a double click on the formula in the Formula bar. The Formula bar is nothing else but the text editor of the source code.

The coding of Task 2

$$\{=\text{LEN}(A2:A51)\} \tag{4}$$

$$\{=\text{LEN}(A2:A51)-1\} \tag{5}$$

$$\{=\text{RIGHT}(A2:A51,\text{LEN}(A2:A51)-1)\} \tag{6}$$

Table 3: The output values of the formulas solving Task 2

States	F4	F5	F6
Alabama	8	7	Alabama
Alaska	7	6	Alaska
Maryland	9	8	Maryland
Massachusetts[D]	17	16	Massachusetts[D]
Oregon	7	6	Oregon
Pennsylvania[E]	16	15	Pennsylvania[E]
Vermont	8	7	Vermont
Virginia[G]	12	11	Virginia[G]
Washington	11	10	Washington
West Virginia	14	13	West Virginia
Wisconsin	10	9	Wisconsin
Wyoming	8	7	Wyoming

Remove the accidental [X] string from the end of the names of the states (Figure 4, Table 4).

The characteristics of Task 3

– Not all the strings have [X] (D).

– The names have different length (D).

– The [X] is on the right side of the name (S).

– The [X] string is three-character-long (S).

– The [X] string starts with a [character (S).

The algorithm of Task 3

– Deciding the positon of [(Formula 7)

– Checking the presence or lack of [(Formula 8)

– Question for the presence or lack of [(Formula 9) (the true branch of the IF() function is substituted with the empty string)

– If there is no [X] string then write out the Space-free string, which comes from Formula 6 (Formula 10)

– If there is an [X] string then cut out the left side of the Space-free string, to the left of the [character (Formula 11 or 12)

The coding of Task 3

{=SEARCH("[",A2:A51)}   (7)

{=ISERROR(SEARCH("[",A2:A51))}   (8)

{=IF(ISERROR(SEARCH("[",A2:A51)),"")}   (9)

{=IF(ISERROR(SEARCH("[",A2:A51)),RIGHT(A2:A51,LEN(A2:A51)-1))} (10)

{=IF(ISERROR(SEARCH("[",A2:A51)),RIGHT(A2:A51,LEN(A2:A51)-1),
LEFT(RIGHT(A2:A51,LEN(A2:A51)-1),SEARCH("[",A2:A51)-2))}   (11)

{=IF(ISERROR(SEARCH("[",A2:A51)),RIGHT(A2:A51,LEN(A2:A51)-1),
LEFT(RIGHT(A2:A51,LEN(A2:A51)-1),LEN(A2:A51)-4))}   (12)

Table 4: The output values of the formulas solving Task 3

States	F7	F8	F9	F10	F11 or F12
Alabama	#VALUE!	TRUE		Alabama	Alabama
Alaska	#VALUE!	TRUE		Alaska	Alaska
Maryland	#VALUE!	TRUE		Maryland	Maryland
Massachusetts[D]	15	FALSE	FALSE	FALSE	Massachusetts
Oregon	#VALUE!	TRUE		Oregon	Oregon
Pennsylvania[E]	14	FALSE	FALSE	FALSE	Pennsylvania
Vermont	#VALUE!	TRUE		Vermont	Vermont
Virginia[G]	10	FALSE	FALSE	FALSE	Virginia
Washington	#VALUE!	TRUE		Washington	Washington
West Virginia	#VALUE!	TRUE		West Virginia	West Virginia
Wisconsin	#VALUE!	TRUE		Wisconsin	Wisconsin
Wyoming	#VALUE!	TRUE		Wyoming	Wyoming

4.3.2. Single-result array formulas

Single-result array formulas are those whose output is one value, but inside the formulas non-default array(s) are used as arguments.

	A	B	C	D	E	F	G	H	I	J	K	L	M	N	O	P
1	Year	Week	Date	M_5 (No.)	M_5 (Ft)	M_4 (No.)	M_4 (Ft)	M_3 (No.)	M_3 (Ft)	M_2 (No.)	M_2 (Ft)	Ball numbers				
2	2014	33	2014.08.16	0	0 Ft	24	2 332 290 Ft	2632	22 520 Ft	77170	1 495 Ft	6	52	57	68	86
3	2014	32	2014.08.09	1	97 974 140 Ft	43	1 291 130 Ft	2713	21 670 Ft	75043	1 525 Ft	20	28	47	51	71
4	2014	31	2014.08.02	1	192 866 270 Ft	16	3 443 595 Ft	1707	34 175 Ft	61199	1 855 Ft	23	60	76	84	86
5	2014	30	2014.07.26	0	0 Ft	46	1 178 115 Ft	3991	14 380 Ft	98165	1 135 Ft	6	15	22	33	44
513	2004	44		0	0 Ft	27	1 636 218 Ft	2770	16 887 Ft	101002	901 Ft	56	67	72	75	80
514	2004	43		1	152 800 684 Ft	22	1 837 280 Ft	2513	17 031 Ft	82727	1 006 Ft	1	27	29	74	78
868	1998	2		1	47 708 148 Ft	14	1 392 092 Ft	1606	12 135 Ft	59881	570 Ft	1	14	46	59	64
869	1998	1		0	0 Ft	69	270 685 Ft	5090	3 669 Ft	124921	262 Ft	4	18	21	24	29
870	1997	52		0	0 Ft	0	0 Ft	0	0 Ft	0	0 Ft	22	33	45	66	81
871	1997	51		0	0 Ft	0	0 Ft	0	0 Ft	0	0 Ft	1	5	13	55	78
2998	1957	11		0	0 Ft	0	0 Ft	0	0 Ft	0	0 Ft	1	49	64	67	71
2999	1957	10		0	0 Ft	0	0 Ft	0	0 Ft	0	0 Ft	16	61	71	77	89

Figure 6: The sample table of the Hungarian lottery [89]

The sample table in Figure 6 shows the dates of the draws, the prizes (columns E, G, I, and K), the number of the winners (columns D, F, H, and J), and the winning ball numbers (columns L–P) of the lottery played in Hungary. The dates are recorded from the 45th week of 2004 (row 512) and the prizes from the 1st week of 1998 (row 869).

24

To solve Task 4 we have to calculate the sum product of two vectors: M_5 (No.) and M_5 (Ft), columns D and E, respectively.

However, this is a case in which you can avoid introducing a new built-in function. This problem can be solved with a single-result array formula, and there is no need for the built-in SUMPRODUCT() function.

The characteristics of Task 4

–   The number of the winners and prizes are stored in two vectors.

–   The number of the winners and prizes are paired.

The algorithm of Task 4

–   Calculating the products of the numbers of the winners and the prizes. The output is a vector. There is no need to display all the components of the vector; consequently, we only display the first component of the vector, which appears in the cell of the formula (Formula 13).

–   Summing the components of the vector of the products (Formula 14).

We have to note here, however, that if we wish to check the correctness of the vector (Formula 13) we always have the opportunity to create array value results on the worksheet.

The coding of Task 4

$\{=D2:D869*E2:E869\}$ (13)

$\{=SUM(D2:D869*E2:E869)\}$ (14)

The generalization of the problem is detailed in Task 12.

Task 5:	Calculate the square sum of the differences of the number of the winners and the average of the number of the winners for those who have 2 matches (Figure 6, Table 5).

The characteristics of Task 5

- The number of the winners has to be compared to a calculated value, which in this case is the average of the number of the winners.
- The output is a single value, the square sum of the differences.

The algorithm of Task 5

- Calculating the average of the numbers of winners (Formula 15). The result is a real number.
- Calculating the difference between the components of the vector and the average (Formula 16). The result is a vector. The first component of the vector is displayed in the cell of the formula.
- Calculating the square of the components of the vector from the previous step (Formula 17). The first component of the vector is displayed.
- Summing the components of the vector (Formula 18). The result is a real number.

The coding of Task 5

=AVERAGE (J2:J869)   (15)

{=J2:J869-AVERAGE(J2:J869)}   (16)

{=(J2:J869-AVERAGE(J2:J869))^2}   (17)

{=SUM((J2:J869-AVERAGE(J2:J869))^2)}}   (18)

Since the ultimate output of a single-result array formula is one value, there is no need to display all the items of the array during the consecutive steps of building the formula. In this case the one value or the first item of the array is displayed in the cell of the formula (Table 5). One further advantage of not displaying all the items of the arrays is that the size of the spreadsheet documents can be reduced.

Table 5: The output values of the formulas solving Task 5

Match 2 (No.)	F15	F16	F17	F18
77 170	110 121,8	-32 951,8	1 085 821 624	1 780 096 622 741

Similar single-result formulas can be created with array formulas to solve other problems. If we are aware of this technique, we can again realize that many of the built-in functions of the spreadsheet programs are completely unnecessary (SUMSQ(), SUMX2MY2(), SUMX2PY2(), SUMXMY2()).

4.3.3. Conditional array formulas

Conditional array formulas are the combinations of the methods previously detailed. The main characteristic of these formulas is that there is a condition(s) nested in the multilevel formula. Based on the selection of the condition, different output vectors serve as the argument of the outside function.

	A	B	C	D	E
1	Country	Continent	Capital	Area	Population (thousand)
2	Afghanistan	Asia	Kabul	647500	27756
3	Albania	Europe	Tirana	28748	3545
4	Algeria	Africa	Algiers	2381740	32278
5	American Samoa	Oceania	Pago Pago	199	69
6	Andorra	Europe	Andorra la Vella	468	68
7	Angola	Africa	Luanda	1246700	10593
8	Anguilla	Amerika	The Valley	102	12
233	Yemen	Asia	Sanaa	527970	18701
234	Yugoslavia	Europe	Belgrade	102350	10657
235	Zambia	Africa	Lusaka	752614	9959
236	Zimbabwe	Africa	Harare	390580	11377

Figure 7: The sample table of the countries of the Earth

Task 6:   Give a continent in G2. Find the number of countries in the G2 continent (Figure 7, Table 6).

The characteristics of Task 6

–   Countries which are in the G2 continent should be counted, and the counter should be incremented when there is a matching country.

27

- Countries which are not in the G2 continent should be ignored.

This is a classical looping task with an IF structure inside the loop.

The algorithm of Task 6

- We have to decide whether the continents of the countries match the given continent or not. This can be carried out with one IF() function. The first argument of the IF() function holds the question; however, when using an array formula, not just one question, but many are included (Formula 19). The number of the questions equals the number of the components of the vector, and consequently the number of the output values.
- If the answer is yes to a question, a 1 should be stored (Formula 20).
- If the answer is no to a question, we ignore it, and in this case the default FALSE value is stored (Formula 20).
- The result of the IF() function is a vector whose components are 1s or FALSEs (Formula 20). Similarly to the previous tasks there is no need to display the whole vector, the first component of the vector appears in the cell.
- Finally, we have to count the number of 1s in the output vector (Formula 21). The result is a whole number.

The coding of Task 6

$$\{=\text{B2:B236}=\text{G2}\} \qquad (19)$$

$$\{=\text{IF}(\text{B2:B236}=\text{G2},1)\} \qquad (20)$$

$$\{=\text{SUM}(\text{IF}(\text{B2:B236}=\text{G2},1))\} \qquad (21)$$

It is worth adding a title to each task. For Task 6 a suitable title is constructed in (Formula 22). Again, this is a classical novice programming task, but more meaningful than the "Hello World!" task.

$$=\text{"The number of the countries in "}\&\text{G2} \qquad (22)$$

In Formula 22 a string and a variable are concatenated with the concatenating operator. There is no need for the CONCATENATE() function, consequently it is an absolutely unnecessary function.

Task 7:	Give a number in H2. Tell the population of those countries whose area is greater than H2 (Figure 7).

Task 6 and Task 7 share the same characteristics and algorithm. There are only minor differences.

- There is a question to both tasks (compare Formula 19 to Formula 23).
- While in Task 6 we collected and added 1s, in Task 7 we collect the populations of the countries and add these values (compare Formula 20 to Formula 24 and Formula 21 to Formula 25).

Apart from these two minor differences, nothing has changed, and most importantly, the structure of the two solutions is the same.

The coding of Task 7

$\{=\text{D2:D236}>\text{H2}\}$ (23)

$\{-\text{IF}(\text{D2:D236}>\text{H2},\text{E2.E236})\}$ (24)

$\{=\text{SUM}(\text{IF}(\text{D2:D236}>\text{H2},\text{E2:E236}))\}$ (25)

Table 7: The output values of the formulas solving Task 7 with two different values in H2

Country	Area	H2	F23	F24	F25
Afghanistan	647 500	600	TRUE	27 756	5 989 991
Afghanistan	647 500	700 000	FALSE	FALSE	4 121 077

The title of Task 7 is presented in Formula 26).

="The population of countries whose area is greater than "
&H2&" km²."   (26)

Task 8:	Give two numbers in H2 and I2. Find the average population of those countries whose area is between the values in H2 and I2 (Figure 7, Table 8).

Again, the structure is the same as we have seen in the two previous tasks. The differences are the following.

–   The question is complex; we have to create it with an AND connection (Formula 27 or 28).
–   The output value is an average (Formula 29 or 30 and the extended Formula 32 or 33).
–   We have to be aware of the possibility that both cells could hold either the smaller or the greater number (Formula 32 or 33 and Formula 34).

The algorithm of Task 8 contains the formation of the AND connection. There are two options to create the AND connection.

–   Embedding IF() functions (Formula 27 or 32).
–   Multiplying the two sets within one IF() function (Formula 28 or 33).

The coding of Task 8

$$\{=IF(D2:D236>H2,IF(D2:D236<I2,E2:E236))\} \qquad (27)$$

$$\{=IF((D2:D236>H2)*(D2:D236<I2),E2:E236)\} \qquad (28)$$

$$\{=AVERAGE(IF(D2:D236>H2,IF(D2:D236<I2,E2:E236)))\} \qquad (29)$$

$$\{=AVERAGE(IF((D2:D236>H2)*(D2:D236<I2),E2:E236))\} \qquad (30)$$

Table 8: The output values of the formulas solving Task 8 with different values in H2 and I2

Country	Area	H2	I2	F27 or F28	F29 or F30
Afghanistan	647 500	600	1 500	FALSE	1079.5
Afghanistan	647 500	500 000	700 000	27 756	29 990.6

The title text of Task 8 is in Formula 31.

$$="The\ average\ population\ of\ those\ countries\ whose\ area\ is\ between\ "$$
$$\&H2\&"\ and\ "\&I2\&"\ km^2." \qquad (31)$$

For a further improvement of the solution we have to consider which cell holds the smaller, and which the greater, number; consequently both Formula 29 and 30 can be further modified. The simplest solution is that instead of the plain H2 and I2 variables

30

the smaller and the greater values will be used, respectively. Consequently, the same is true for the title.

$$\{=\text{AVERAGE}(\text{IF}(D2:D236>\text{MIN}(H2,I2),$$
$$\text{IF}(D2:D236<\text{MAX}(H2,I2),E2:E236)))\} \tag{32}$$

$$\{=\text{AVERAGE}(\text{IF}((D2:D236>\text{MIN}(H2,I2))*(D2:D236<\text{MAX}(H2,I2)),$$
$$E2:E236))\} \tag{33}$$

The modified title text of Task 8 is in Formula 34.

$$=\text{"The average population of those countries whose area}$$
$$\text{is between "\&MIN}(H2,I2)\&\text{" and "\&MAX}(H2,I2)\&\text{" km}^2.\text{"} \tag{34}$$

We can also create OR and XOR connections with the built in IF() functions or with operations of sets. The coding is carried out in a similar way to the AND connection. We have to note here that in the conditional built-in functions only the AND connection is included (for details see Section 4.3.4).

Task 9:	Give a continent in G2. Find the capital city of the largest country in the G2 continent (Figure 7, Table 10).

The algorithm of Task 9

- Separating the countries in G2 from the others (Formula 35). The output is a vector with the areas of the G2 countries and FALSEs.
- Selecting the largest area of this vector (Formula 36). The output is a number from the vector of the areas.
- Finding the index of this component of the vector (Formula 37). The output is an index, a whole number.
- Finding the capital city with the same index in the vector of the capital cities (Formula 38).

Before providing the solution to Task 9, we have to draw attention to the fact that the Sprego groups of functions (Table 1) include only the INDEX() and the MATCH() matrix functions. This is intentional, since these two functions are general purpose functions, while the other popular functions are troublesome, and are not worth using.

31

The comparison of the INDEX(MATCH()) multilevel functions and the HLOOKUP(), VLOOKUP() are detailed in Table 9 [58].

Table 9: The comparison of the INDEX(MATCH()) and the HLOOKUP(), VLOOKUP() functions

INDEX(MATCH())	HLOOKUP(), VLOOKUP()
Search vector	
− search both in rows and columns	− HLOOKUP(): searches only in columns − VLOOKUP(): searches only in rows
Result vector	
− can be anywhere in the table	− HLOOKUP(): the search row or below the search row − VLOOKUP(): the search column or right to the search column
The orders of the values in the search vector	
− ascending (default) − descending − no order	− ascending (default) − descending (not available) − no order
The output	
− one value (default) − one vector	− one value (default) − one vector (not available)

To solve Task 9 VLOOKUP() is ruled out, since the data is arranged in columns. HLOOKUP() is ruled out because the output vector is left to the search vector, consequently the only solution is the INDEX(MATCH()) multilevel function (Formulas 37 and 38).

The coding of Task 9

$$\{=IF(B2:B236=G2,D2:D236)\} \tag{35}$$

$$\{=MAX(IF(B2:B236=G2,D2:D236))\} \tag{36}$$

$$\{=MATCH(MAX(IF(B2:B236=G2,D2:D236)),D2:D236,0)\} \tag{37}$$

$$\{=INDEX(C2:C236,MATCH(MAX(IF(B2:B236=G2,D2:D236)),D2:D236,0))\} \tag{38}$$

Table 10: The output values of the formulas solving Task 9 with all the possible continents in G2

Country	G2	F35	F36	F37	F38
Afghanistan	Africa	FALSE	2 505 810	198	Khartoum
Afghanistan	America	FALSE	9 976 140	37	Ottawa
Afghanistan	Asia	647 500	17 075 200	176	Moscow
Afghanistan	Europe	FALSE	2 166 086	84	Nuuk
Afghanistan	Oceania	FALSE	7 686 850	12	Canberra

The title of Task 9 is in Formula 39.

$$="The capital city of the largest country in "\&G2 \tag{39}$$

4.3.4. Advantages of conditional single-result array formulas

As has been presented above, creating conditions with single-result array formulas has many advantages [29].

–   The structure is simple.
    –   There is a condition deep in the formula, coded with an IF() function(s).
    –   The output of the IF() function(s) is an array (Table 12, Step 3).
    –   The output of the IF() function(s) is the argument of a function outside to it (Table 12, Step 4).
–   We use simple general purpose Sprego functions.
–   We handle variables.
–   We can define AND, OR, and XOR connections.
–   We can avoid the use of the troublesome built-in conditional functions: COUNTIF(), COUNTIFS(), SUMIF(), SUMIFS(), AVERAGEIF(), AVERAGEIFS(), COUNTBLANK(), which we refer to as *IF?() functions [59], [73]:
    –   *IF?() functions are not compatible; they vary from program to program, and from version to version.
    –   *IF?() functions use different syntactic rules for the constants and the variables, and for equality and inequality (compare Table 11 and Table 13),
    –   *IF?() functions handle only the AND connection.

33

- In the *IF?() functions no embedded functions are allowed.
- The order of the arguments are different of functions with similar purposes (compare the two solutions in Table 13).
- There is no need for the database functions [39], whose usage requires some kind of data-management- knowledge, which novices do not have.

The examples have proved that problems similar to those presented to novices in high level languages can be solved with Sprego functions. There is no need for the problem-specific problem loaded built-in functions. We can work more effectively, and more problems can be solved with the simple general purpose functions. Beyond the obvious advantages of the Sprego functions, most importantly, we have to notice that students' algorithmic skills are developed by building the algorithms for the given problems, and they carry out real data retrieval.

4.4. Debugging

There is one more tool which works effectively with Sprego functions and Sprego programming; this is debugging. The importance of debugging in spreadsheet languages is as great as in any other programming language; however, built-in functions do not support debugging. They do not allow any insight into the algorithms behind the functions. This drawback of the built-in functions is another source of error-prone documents.

For debugging it is worth cropping the table to a reasonable size, for at least two reasons. First of all, checking tens and hundreds of values is tiresome, boring, time-consuming and makes it difficult to find the essence of the problem. The other problem with long arrays is that the debugging window is small, not of a convenient size, not re-sizeable, and data cannot be copied from it.

When using the built-in *IF?() functions the steps of the evaluation are hidden from the user (Table 11 and Table 13); there are no options for debugging and analyzing the process of the evaluation of the formulas. The results of the *IF?() functions are presented in one step, without any traces of the algorithms lying behind them.

Table 11: The debugging of the COUNTIF() function solving Task 6

	=COUNTIF(B2:B8,G2)
1.	COUNTIF(B2:B8,G2)
2.	2

Table 12: A comparison of the debugging of the SUM(IF()) and AVERAGE(IF()) array formulas

	The number of countries in G2 continent (Task 6).	The average population of those countries whose area is smaller than H2 (Task 8).
	{=SUM(IF(B2:B8=G2,1))}	{=AVERAGE(IF(D2:D8<H2,E2:E8))}
1.	SUM(IF(B2:B8=G2,1))	AVERAGE(IF(D2:D8<H2,E2:E8))
2.	SUM(IF({"Asia","Europe","Africa", "Oceania","Europe","Africa", "America"}="Africa",1))	AVERAGE(IF({647500,28748, 2381740,199,468,1246700,102} <600,E2:E8))
3.	SUM(IF({FALSE,FALSE,TRUE,FALSE, FALSE,TRUE,FALSE},1))	AVERAGE(IF({FALSE,FALSE,FALSE, TRUE,TRUE,FALSE,TRUE},E2:E8))
4.	SUM({FALSE,FALSE,1,FALSE,FALSE, 1,FALSE})	AVERAGE({FALSE,FALSE,FALSE,69, 68,FALSE,12})

The other advantage of the conditional single-result array formulas is that their structures constitute similar problems, so the steps of the evaluation process of this kind of multilevel function is also similar (Table 12). One of the most important steps is Step 3 in Table 12, which presents the output vector of the IF() function. This vector serves as the argument of the outside function SUM() and AVERAGE() (Table 12, Task 6 and Task 8, respectively).

Table 13: A comparison of the argument-list and the evaluation steps of the built-in functions AVERAGEIF() and AVERAGEIFS()

	=AVERAGEIF(D2:D8,"<"&H2,E2:E8)	=AVERAGEIFS(E2:E8,D2:D8,"<"&H2)
1.	AVERAGEIF(D2:D8,"<"&H2,E2:E8)	AVERAGEIFS(E2:E8,D2:D8,"<"&H2)
2.	AVERAGEIF($D$2:$D$8,"<"&600, E2:E8)	AVERAGEIFS(E2:E8,D2:D8,"<"&600)
3.	AVERAGEIF($D$2:$D$8,"<600", E2:E8)	AVERAGEIFS($E$2:$E$8,$D$2:$D$8,"<" &600)
4.	49.66666667	49.66666667

5. Conclusions

Based on previously published results, the high expectations placed on spreadsheet programming have been partially realized; spreadsheets are extremely popular. On the other hand, we are faced with the side effects of this popularity, namely, the unexpectedly high number of error-prone documents, causing serious financial losses.

We have proved that the lack of deep approach metacognitive problem solving methods has led us to misuse spreadsheets. The most widely accepted methods for solving spreadsheet problems is the TAEW-based surface approach method, which lacks the skills required to solve computer related activities, i.e. to build algorithms.

Considering the advantages of the spreadsheet languages, we have invented a programming method which would serve as an introductory language for programmers and as the ultimate language for end-user programmers, which we have named Sprego.

Sprego is a deep approach metacognitive problem solving environment, which has borrowed and combined proven methods from high level programming languages. The five milestones of Sprego are

- using as few and as simple general purpose functions as possible,
- building multilevel formulas,
- building array formulas,
- debugging,
- using authentic tables.

With this approach the requirements of the deep approach metacognitive methods are fulfilled (H1).

In addition to building the theoretical background we had to find the tools which are needed to carry out our H1 hypothesis. Spreadsheets have a long-established, built-in, but hardly used feature, the array formulas, which suit our requirements. As has been presented in the previous sections, with array formulas we can solve problems well known and well accepted in teaching programming to novices (H3). The few simple

36

general purpose functions for creating the formulas do not require the service of the GUI; it is much more convenient to build and expand the array formulas by typing and coding than by wandering around in the GUI (H3). On the other hand, the advantage of the GUI is obvious, and makes the programming more convenient for novices, both when defining the variables and arrays, and when handling large tables.

Based on the minimalist approach which supports Sprego, the differences between the various spreadsheet programs and versions are eliminated. Using Sprego there is no need to check the versions of the programs, and, furthermore, there is free transportation of formulas between MS Excel and OpenOffice, LibreOffice Calc (H4).

Since Sprego mainly relies on simple general purpose functions, and these functions are frequently used, the users get used to them in a short period of time and make fewer errors than in the rarely used, problem-specific functions, with their strange syntactic rules and lists of arguments. Beyond this, the usage of array formulas eliminates the errors caused by copying formulas (H5).

Altogether, we have found a programming language and technique which could serve as an introductory language and the language of those who do not want to be professional programmers, i.e. end-user programmers. The method and the technique support the development of computational thinking, an ability which is very much required to solve computer related activities, and for effective human computer interaction.

6. Bibliography

[1]   Abraham, R. and Erwig, M. (2006) Type inference for spreadsheets. In Proceedings of the 8th ACM SIGPLAN international conference on Principles and practice of declarative programming, http://web.engr.oregonstate.edu/~erwig/papers/TypeInf_PPDP06.pdf, accessed 15-July-2014.

[2]   Abraham, R. and Erwig, M. (2009) Mutation Operators for Spreadsheets. *IEEE Transactions on Software Engineering*, 35(1), pp. 94–108.

[3]   Angeli, C. (2013) Teaching spreadsheets: A TPCK perspective. In Kadijevich, Dj. M., Angeli, C., and Schulte, C. (Eds.). 2013. *Improving Computer Science Education.* New York and London: Routledge; pp. 132–145.

[4]   Ben-Ari, M. (1999) Bricolage Forever! PPIG 1999. 11th Annual Workshop. 5–7 January 1999. Computer-Based Learning Unit, University of Leeds, UK. http://www.ppig.org/papers/11th-benari.pdf, accessed 12-April-2014.

[5]   Ben-Ari, M. and Yeshno, T. (2006) Conceptual models of software artifacts. *Interacting with Computers,* Volume 18, Issue 6, December 2006, pp. 1336–1350.

[6]   Ben-Ari, M. (2011) Non-myths about programming. Proceeding. ICER '10 Proceedings of the Sixth international workshop on Computing education research. July 2011 | Vol. 54 | No. 7 | *Communications of the ACM.*

[7]   Biró, P. and Csernoch, M. (2013) Deep and surface structural metacognitive abilities of the first year students of Informatics. 4th IEEE International Conference on Cognitive Info-communications, Proceedings, Budapest, pp. 521–526.

[8]   Biró, P. and Csernoch, M. (2013) Programming skills of the first year students of Informatics. XXIII. International Conference on Computer Science 2013, EMT, in Hungarian, pp. 154–159.

[9]   Biró, P. and Csernoch, M. (2014) An Algorithmic Approach to Spreadsheets, in Hungarian, Interdiszciplináris pedagógia és a fenntartható fejlődés. Szerk.: Buda András, Kiss Endre, DE Neveléstudományok Intézete, Debrecen, 310-321, 2014. ISBN: 9789634737308

[10]   Biró, P. and Csernoch, M. (2014) Deep and surface metacognitive processes in non-traditional programming tasks. In: 5th IEEE International Conference on Cognitive Infocommunications CogInfoCom 2014 Proceedings. IEEE Catalog Number: CFP1426R-USB, Vietri sul Mare, Italy, 49-54, 2014. ISBN: 9781479972791.

[11]   Biró P. and Csernoch M. (2014): Students' Knowledge in Informatics from the Students' and the Teachers' Perspectives. In Hungarian, Informatika szakos hallgatok tudására vonatkozó tudásmerés tanári es hallgatói megközelítésben. In: Minőség és versenyképes tudás: Neveléstudományi konferencia 2013. Szerk.: Demény Piroska, Foris-Ferenczi Rita, BBTE, Pedagógia es Alkalmazott Didaktika Intézet, Kolozsvár, 165-172, 2014. ISBN: 9789730163414.

[12]   Biró, P., Csernoch, M., Abari, K., Máth, J. (2014) First year students' algorithmic skills in tertiary Computer Science education. In: Proceedings of the 9th International Conference on Knowledge, Information and Creativity Support Systems, Limassol, Cyprus, November 6-8, 2014. Ed.: George Angelos Papadopoulos, Cyprus Library, Cyprus, 301-306, 2014. ISBN: 9789963700844.

[13] Booth, S. (1992) Learning to program: A phenomenographic perspective. Gothenburg, Sweden: Acta Universitatis Gothoburgensis.

[14] Bransford, J.D., Brown, A.L. and Cocking, R.R., Ed. (2004) How People Learn: Brain, Mind, Experience, and School, Washington, D.C.: National Academy Press.

[15] Calculation operators and precedence 2013. http://office.microsoft.com/en-us/excel-help/calculation-operators-and-precedence-HP010342223.aspx, accessed 12-April-2014.

[16] Carroll, J.M. (1990) The Nurnberg funnel: designing minimalist instruction for practical computer skill, M.I.T. Press, Cambridge, Mass.

[17] Case, J.M. (2000) Students' perceptions of context, approaches to learning and metacognitive development in a second year chemical engineering course. Unpublished PhD, Monash University, Melbourne.

[18] Case, J.M. and Gunstone, R.F. (2002) Metacognitive development as a shift in approach to learning: an in-depth study. *Studies in Higher Education*, 27(4), pp. 459–470.

[19] Case, J.M. and Gunstone, R.F. (2003) Approaches to learning in a second year chemical engineering course. *International Journal of Science Education*, 25(7), pp. 801–819.

[20] Case, J.M., Gunstone, R.F. and Lewis, A. (2001) Students' metacognitive development in an innovative second year chemical engineering course, Research in Science Education, 31(3), pp. 331–355.

[21] Computer Science Curricula 2013. Curriculum Guidelines for Undergraduate Degree Programs in Computer Science. December 20, 2013. The Joint Task Force on Computing Curricula Association for Computing Machinery (ACM) IEEE Computer Society. http://www.acm.org/education/CS2013-final-report.pdf, accessed 12-April-2014.

[22] Cox, M. T. (2005) Metacognition in computation: A selected research review. *Artificial Intelligence*, 169 (2), pp. 104–141.

[23] Create conditional formulas. http://office.microsoft.com/en-us/excel-help/create-conditional-formulas-HP005251012.aspx, accessed 1-June-2014.

[24] Creating formulas 2011. Last modified 5 January, 2011. http://wiki.openoffice.org/wiki/Documentation/OOo3_User_Guides/Calc_Guide/Creating_for mulas#Operators_in_formulas, accessed 12-April-2014.

[25] Csernoch, M. (1997) Methodological Questions of Teaching Word Processing. 3rd International Conference on Applied Informatics: Eger-Noszvaj, Hungary, August 25–28, 1997, pp. 375–382.

[26] Csernoch, M. (2009) Teaching word processing – the theory behind. *Teaching Mathematics and Computer Science,* 2009/1. pp. 119–137.

[27]   Csernoch, M. (2010) Teaching word processing – the practice. *Teaching Mathematics and Computer Science*, 8/2 (2010). pp. 247–262.

[28]   Csernoch, M. (2012) Introducing Conditional Array Formulas in Spreadsheet Classes. EDULEARN12 Proceedings. Barcelona, Spain. 2-4 July, 2012. Publisher: IATED, pp. 7270–7279.

[29]   Csernoch, M. (2014) Programming with Spreadsheet Functions: Sprego. In Hungarian, Programozás táblázatkezelő függvényekkel – Sprego. Műszaki Könyvkiadó, Budapest.

[30]   Csernoch, M. and Balogh, L. (2010) Algorithms and Spreadsheet-management – Talent Support In Education In The Field Of Informatics. In Hungarian, Algoritmusok és táblázatkezelés – Tehetséggondozás a közoktatásban az informatika területén. Association of Hungarian Talent Support Organizations, in Hungarian, Magyar Tehetségsegítő Szervezetek Szövetsége, Budapest. ISSN: 2062-5936
http://tehetseg.hu/sites/default/files/16_kotet_net_color.pdf, accessed 15-July-2014.

[31]   Csernoch, M. and Biró, P. (2013) The investigation of the effectiveness of Bottom-up techniques in the spreadsheet education of students of Informatics. In Hungarian Button-up technikák hatékonyságának vizsgálata informatika szakos hallgatók táblázatkezelés-oktatásában. (Eds): Kozma T. and Perjés I., New Research in Education Studies. ELTE Eötvös Publisher, Budapest. pp. 369–392.

[32]   Csernoch, M. and Biró, P. (2013) Teachers' Assessment and Students' Self-Assessment on the Students' Spreadsheet Knowledge. EDULEARN13 Proceedings 5th International Conference on Education and New Learning Technologies July 1st-3rd, 2013 — Barcelona, Spain. Edited by L. Gómez Chova, A. López Martínez, I. Candel Torres. International Association of Technology, Education and Development. IATED. ISBN: 978-84-616-3822-2. pp. 949–956.

[33]   Csernoch, M. and Biró, P. (2014) Spreadsheet misconceptions, spreadsheet errors. Oktatáskutatás határon innen és túl. *HERA Évkönyvek* I., ed. Juhász Erika, Kozma Tamás, Publisher: Belvedere Meridionale, Szeged, (2014), 370–395.

[34]   Csernoch, M. and Biró, P. (2014) Digital Competency and Digital Literacy is at Stake, ECER 2014 Conference, 1–5. September, 2014, Porto, Portugal. http://www.eera-ecer.de/ecer-programmes/conference/19/contribution/31885/, accessed 12-October-2014.

[35]   Csernoch, M. Biró, P., Máth, J. and Abari, K. (2014) What do I know in Informatics? In Hungarian, Mit tudok informatikából?. IF2014 Conference, 27–29 August, 2014, Debrecen, Hungary. ISBN 978-963-473-712-4, pp. 217-230.

[36]   Csernoch, M. and Bujdosó, Gy. (2009) Quality text editing. *Journal of Computer Science and Control Systems*. 2/2 pp. 5–10.

40

[37] Csernoch, M., Simon, K., Brósch, É., and Kiss, É. (2014) I Have Learned Spreadsheet Management With Sprego. In Hungarian, Spregoval tanultam táblázatkezelést. In: Zsakó László (szerk.) INFO Éra 2014. Zamárdi, Magyarország, 2014.11.20-2014.11.22. Budapest: NJSZT, pp. 1–20. ISBN 978-963-12-0627-2. http://people.inf.elte.hu/szlavi/InfoDidact14/Manuscripts/CsM_SK_BE_KE.pdf, accessed 15-December-2014.

[38] Csíkos, Cs. (2006) Metacognition. The pedagogy of knowledge referring to knowledge. In Hungarian, Metakogníció – A tudásra vonatkozó tudás pedagógiája. Műszaki Könyvkiadó, Budapest.

[39] Database functions 2010. http://office.microsoft.com/en-us/excel-help/excel-functions-by-category-HP010342656.aspx#BMdatabase_functions, accessed 15-December-2013.

[40] Digital literacy in education. (2011) UNESCO Institute for Information Technologies. http://unesdoc.unesco.org/images/0021/002144/214485e.pdf, accessed 15-December-2013.

[41] EuSpRig, European Spreadsheet Risks Interest Group. http://www.eusprig.org/, accessed 15-December-2013.

[42] Elliott, C. M. (2007) Tangible Functional Programming. ICFP'07, October 1–3, 2007, Freiburg, Germany. http://conal.net/papers/Eros/eros.pdf, accessed 15-June-2014.

[43] Glaser, H., Hankin, C. and Till, D. (1984) Principles of functional programming. London: Prentice Hall.

[44] Gove, M. (2012) Michael Gove speech at the BETT Show 2012. Published 13 January 2012. https://www.gov.uk/government/speeches/michael-gove-speech-at-the-bett-show-2012, accessed 15-June-2014.

[45] Gove, M. (2014) Michael Gove speaks about computing and education technology. Published 22 January 2014. https://www.gov.uk/government/speeches/michael-gove-speaks-about-computing-and-education-technology, accessed 15-June-2014.

[46] IF. https://wiki.openoffice.org/wiki/Documentation/How_Tos/Calc:_IF_function, accessed 1-June-2014.

[47] IF. https://help.libreoffice.org/Calc/Logical_Functions#IF, accessed 1-June-2014.

[48] IF function. http://office.microsoft.com/en-us/excel-help/if-function-HP010342586.aspx?CTT=5&origin=HA010342655, accessed 1-June-2014.

[49] Informatics education: Europe cannot afford to miss the boat. Report of the joint Informatics Europe & ACM Europe Working Group on Informatics Education April 2013. http://germany.acm.org/upload/pdf/ACMandIEreport.pdf, accessed 15-June-2014.

[50] Kruger, J. and Dunning, D. (1999) Unskilled and Unaware of It: How Difficulties in Recognizing One's Own Incompetence Lead to Inflated Self-Assessments. *Journal of Personality and Social Psychology* 77 (6): pp. 1121–34.

[51] Jorgensen, H. (2013) How not to Excel in economics http://www.lowyinterpreter.org/post/2013/04/18/How-not-to-Excel-in-economics.aspx, accessed 15-June-2014.

[52] Kadijevich, Dj. (2009) Simple spreadsheet modeling by first-year business undergraduate students: Difficulties in the transition from real world problem statement to mathematical model. In M. Blomhřj and S. Carreira (Eds.), Mathematical applications and modeling in the teaching and learning of mathematics: Proceedings the 11th International Congress on mathematical Education, Mexico, pp. 241–248.

[53] Kadijevich, Dj. (2013) Learning about spreadsheet. In Kadijevich, Dj. M., Angeli, C., and Schulte, C. (Eds.). (2013). *Improving Computer Science Education*. New York and London: Routledge, pp. 19–33.

[54] Kirschner, P.A., Sweller, J., Clark, R.E. (2006) Why Minimal Guidance During Instruction Does Not Work: An Analysis of the Failure of Constructivist Discovery, Problem-Based, Experiential, and Inquiry-Based Teaching. *Educational Psychologist*, 41(2), pp. 75–86.

[55] Koriat, A. and Levy-Sadot, R. (2000) Conscious and Unconscious Metacognition: A Rejoinder. *Consciousness and Cognition*. (9). pp. 193–202.

[56] Kwak, J. (2013) The Importance of Excel. http://baselinescenario.com/2013/02/09/the-importance-of-excel, accessed 15-June-2014.

[57] Lister, R., Adams, E.S., Fitzgerald, S., Fone, W., Hamer, J., Lindholm, M., McCartney, R., Moström, J.E., Sanders, K., Seppälä, O., Simon, B. and Thomas, L. (2004) A multi-national study of reading and tracing skills in novice programmers., SIGCSE Bull., 2004, vol. 36 (4), pp. 119–150.

[58] Lookup and reference functions 2010. http://office.microsoft.com/en-us/excel-help/excel-functions-by-category-HP010342656.aspx#BMlookup_and_reference_functions, accessed 15-June-2014.

[59] Math and trigonometry functions 2010. http://office.microsoft.com/en-us/excel-help/excel-functions-by-category-HP010342656.aspx#BMmath_and_trigonometry_functions, accessed 15-June-2014.

[60] Mayer, R. E. (1981) The Psychology of How Novices Learn Computer Programming. *ACM Computing Surveys*, vol. 13 (1), pp. 121–141.

[61] Message, R. (2013) Programming for humans: a new paradigm for domain-specific languages. Technical Report. UCAM-CL-TR-843. ISSN 1476-2986

[62] Nardi, B.A. and Miller, J.R. (1990) The spreadsheet interface: A basis for end-user programming. In D. Diaper et al (Eds.), Human-Computer Interaction: INTERACT '90, Amsterdam, 1990. http://www.miramontes.com/writing/spreadsheet-eup/, accessed 15-June-2014.

[63] Nielsen, J. (1993) Usability Engineering. Academic Press, Boston, MA.

[64] Panko, R.R. (2008) What We Know About Spreadsheet Errors. Journal of End User Computing's. Special issue on Scaling Up End User Development. (10)2, pp. 15–21.

[65] Payton-Jones, S.L, Blackwell, A. and Burnett, M. (2003) A User-Centred Approach to Functions in Excel. International Conference on Functional Programming. (ICFP'03), Uppsala, 2003.

[66] Powell, S.G., Baker, K.R. and Lawson, B. (2008) A critical review of the literature on spreadsheet errors. *Decision Support Systems*, 46(1), pp. 128–138.

[67] Powell, S.G., Baker, K.R. and Lawson, B. (2009) Errors in operational spreadsheets. *Journal of Organizational and End-User Computing*, 1(3), pp. 4–36.

[68] Powell, S.G., Baker, K.R. and Lawson, B. (2009) Impact of errors in operational spreadsheets. *Decision Support Systems*, 47(2), pp. 126–132.

[69] JPMorgan (2013) Report of JPMorgan Chase & Co. Management Task Force. Regarding 2012. CIO Losses. http://files.shareholder.com/downloads/ONE/2272984969x0x628656/4cb574a0-0bf5-4728-9582-625e4519b5ab/Task_Force_Report.pdf, accessed 15-June-2014.

[70] Scaffidi, Ch., Shaw, M. and Myers, B. (2005) Estimating the Numbers of End Users and End User Programmers. In Proceedings of the 2005 IEEE Symposium on Visual Languages and Human-Centric Computing, pp. 207–214.

[71] Sestoft, P. (2011) Spreadsheet technology. Version 0.12 of 2012-01-31. IT University Technical Report ITU-TR-2011-142. IT University of Copenhagen, December 2011.

[72] Sine, R. (2014) Program or Perish: Why Everyone Should Learn to Code. Mar 13, 2014. http://www.coca-colacompany.com/stories/program-or-perish-why-everyone-should-learn-to-code, accessed 15-June-2014.

[73] Statistical functions 2010. http://office.microsoft.com/en-us/excel-help/excel-functions-by-category-HP010342656.aspx#BMstatistical_functions, accessed 15-June-2014.

[74] Soloway, E. (1993) Should we teach students to program? *Communications of the ACM*. October 1993/Vol.36, No.10, pp. 21–24.

[75] Teo, T. and Tan, M. (1999) Spreadsheet Development and "What-if" Analysis: Quantitative versus Qualitative Errors. *Accounting Management and Information Technologies*, vol. 9, pp. 141–160.

43

[76] Tufte, E. R. (2004) The Cognitive Style of PowerPoint: Pitching Out Corrupts Within. Graphics Press.

[77] Tort, F. (2010) Teaching Spreadsheets: Curriculum Design Principles. In S. Thorne (Ed.), Proceedings of the EuSpRIG 2010 conference: Practical steps to protect organisations from out-of-control spreadsheets, pp. 99–110.

[78] Tort, F., Blondel, F.M. and Bruillard É. (2008) Spreadsheet Knowledge and Skills of French Secondary School Students. R.T. Mittermeir and M.M. Sysło (Eds.): ISSEP 2008, LNCS 5090, 305–316, 2008. Springer-Verlag Berlin Heidelberg.

[79] Van Deursen A. and Van Dijk J. (2012) CTRL ALT DELETE. Lost productivity due to IT problems and inadequate computer skills in the workplace. Enschede: Universiteit Twente. http://www.ecdl.org/media/ControlAltDelete_LostProductivityLackofICTSkills_Universtiyof Twente1.pdf, accessed 15-June-2014.

[80] Wakeling, D. (2007) Spreadsheet functional programming. JFP 17(1), pp. 131–143, 2007. Cambridge University Press.

[81] Walkenbach, J. and Wilcox, C. (2003) Putting basic array formulas to work. http://office.microsoft.com/en-us/excel-help/putting-basic-array-formulas-to-work-HA001087292. aspx?CTT=5&origin=HA001087290, accessed 15-June-2014.

[82] Walkenbach, J. (2003) Excel2003 Formulas. John Wiley & Sons.

[83] Warren, P. (2004) Learning to program: spreadsheets, scripting and HCI, in Proceedings of the Sixth Australasian Conference on Computing Education – vol. 30, Darlinghurst, Australia, pp. 327–333.

[84] Wilcox, C. and Walkenbach, J. (2003) Introducing array formulas in Excel. http://office.microsoft.com/en-us/excel-help/introducing-array-formulas-in-excel-HA001087290. aspx, accessed 15-June-2014.

[85] Wing, J. M. (2006) Computational Thinking. March 2006/Vol. 49, No. 3 *Communications of the ACM.*

[86] Zsakó, L. (2006) Combinatorics – Competition – Excel. Teaching Mathematics and Computer Science, 4/2 (2006), pp. 427–435.

7. Sources

[87] Matryoshka doll. http://esemenyhorizont.uw.hu/2009/letfilo/beta01.jpg, accessed 1-June-2012.

[88] List of states and territories of the United States.
http://en.wikipedia.org/wiki/List_of_states_and_territories_of_the_United_States, accessed 1-
June-2014.

[89] The winning numbers of the Hungarian lottery. http://www.szerencsejatek.hu/xls/otos.html,
accessed 20-August-2014.

8. Additional examples in Sprego

To handle strings the table of the states of US would serve as the best task (Figure 2). Column G contains data – the area in mi^2 and km^2 –, which should be separated and stored in two columns, while the numbers preceding the mi^2 should be deleted.

Task 10:   Cut out the km^2 value from its original string (Figure 2).

The characteristics of Task 10

– These numbers are in a pair of parentheses.
– They are on the right of the string.

The output values of the consecutive steps are presented in Table 14. The input values of the problem are in the first column (peach background), while the output values are in the last column (green background). The values presented in the columns are the input values of the consecutive formula, indicated in the first row of the next column.

The algorithm of Task 10

– Finding the position of the opening parenthesis (Formula 40).
– Finding the number of characters which should be cut out from the right side of the original string (Formula 41).
– Cutting out the number and the closing parenthesis from the right (Formula 42).
– Cutting out the left of this new string, which is one character shorter than the previous string (Formula 43).
– Converting the text to number (Formula 44).

45

The coding of Task 10

$$\{=\text{SEARCH}("(",G2:G51)\} \tag{40}$$

$$\{=\text{LEN}(G2:G51)-\text{SEARCH}("(",G2:G51)\} \tag{41}$$

$$\{=\text{RIGHT}(G2:G51,\text{LEN}(G2:G51)-\text{SEARCH}("(",G2:G51))\} \tag{42}$$

$$\{=\text{LEFT}(\text{RIGHT}(G2:G51,\text{LEN}(G2:G51)-\text{SEARCH}("(",G2:G51)),$$
$$\text{LEN}(\text{RIGHT}(G2:G51,\text{LEN}(G2:G51)-\text{SEARCH}("(",G2:G51)))-1)\} \tag{43}$$

$$\{=\text{LEFT}(\text{RIGHT}(G2:G51,\text{LEN}(G2:G51)-\text{SEARCH}("(",G2:G51)),$$
$$\text{LEN}(\text{RIGHT}(G2:G51,\text{LEN}(G2:G51)-\text{SEARCH}("(",G2:G51)))-1)*1\} \tag{44}$$

Table 14: The output values of the formulas solving Task 10

Total area in mi2 (km2)	F40	F41	F42	F43	F44
700452420000000000052,420 (135,767)	27	8	135,767)	135,767	135,767
700566538400000000665,384 (1,723,337)	28	10	1,723,337)	1,723,337	1,723,337
700412406000000000012,406 (32,131)	27	7	32,131)	32,131	32,131
700410554000000000010,554 (27,335)	27	7	27,335)	27,335	27,335
700498379000000000098,379 (254,800)	27	8	254,800)	254,800	254,800
700446054000000000046,054 (119,279)	27	8	119,279)	119,279	119,279
700396160000000009,616 (24,905)	26	7	24,905)	24,905	24,905
700442775000000000042,775 (110,787)	27	8	110,787)	110,787	110,787
700471298000000000071,298 (184,661)	27	8	184,661)	184,661	184,661
700424230000000000024,230 (62,755)	27	7	62,755)	62,755	62,755
700465496000000000065,496 (169,634)	27	8	169,634)	169,634	169,634
700497813000000000097,813 (253,335)	27	8	253,335)	253,335	253,335

Task 11:   Separate the mi^2 value from its original string (Figure 4).

The characteristics of Task 11

- Numbers of different lengths (D).
- Numbers start at the same position: 20 (S).
- mi^2 is left of km^2 (S).

The algorithm of Task 11

- Removing the km^2 from the right of the string (Formula 46).

46

- Finding the position of the opening parenthesis (Formula 45).
- Deciding on the number of characters in the extended mi^2 string, number of characters with the leading 19 characters (Formula 47).
- Deciding on the number of characters in the mi^2 string, number of characters without the leading 19 characters (Formula 48).
- Cutting out mi^2 characters from the right side of string (Formula 46) with formula (Formula 49).
- Converting the text to number (Formula 50).

The output values of the formulas of Task 11 are listed in Table 15.

Table 15: The output values of the formulas solving Task 11

Total area in mi2 (km2)	F45	F46	F47	F48	F49	F50
700452420000000000052,420 (135,767)	27	700452420000000000052,420	25	6	52,420	52,420
700566538400000000665,384 (1,723,337)	28	700566538400000000665,384	26	7	665,384	665,384
700412406000000000012,406 (32,131)	27	700412406000000000012,406	25	6	12,406	12,406
700410554000000000010,554 (27,335)	27	700410554000000000010,554	25	6	10,554	10,554
700498379000000000098,379 (254,800)	27	700498379000000000098,379	25	6	98,379	98,379
700446054000000000046,054 (119,279)	27	700446054000000000046,054	25	6	46,054	46,054
700396160000000009,616 (24,905)	26	700396160000000009,616	24	5	9,616	9,616
700442775000000000042,775 (110,787)	27	700442775000000000042,775	25	6	42,775	42,775
700471298000000000071,298 (184,661)	27	700471298000000000071,298	25	6	71,298	71,298
700424230000000000024,230 (62,755)	27	700424230000000000024,230	25	6	24,230	24,230
700465496000000000065,496 (169,634)	27	700465496000000000065,496	25	6	65,496	65,496
700497813000000000097,813 (253,335)	27	700497813000000000097,813	25	6	97,813	97,813

The coding of Task 11

{=SEARCH("(",G2:G51)} (45)

{=LEFT(G2:G51,SEARCH("(",G2:G51)-2)} (46)

{LEN(LEFT(G2:G51,SEARCH("(",G2:G51)-2))} (47)

{LEN(LEFT(G2:G51,SEARCH("(",G2:G51)-2))-19)} (48)

{=RIGHT(LEFT(G2:G51,SEARCH("(",G2:G51)-2),
LEN(LEFT(G2:G51,SEARCH("(",G2:G51)-2))-19)} (49)

$$\{=\text{RIGHT}(\text{LEFT}(\text{G2:G51},\text{SEARCH}("(",\text{G2:G51})-2),$$

$$\text{LEN}(\text{LEFT}(\text{G2:G51},\text{SEARCH}("(",\text{G2:G51})-2))-19)*1\} \tag{50}$$

The following task is based on Figure 6, the table of the lottery numbers and prizes.

Task 12:	Type the number of the matching balls into R2. Give the total prize for R2 matches (Figure 6).

Task 12 is the generalization of Task 4. The difference between them is that in Task 4 the number of the matches was a constant, as were the columns of the number of winners and the prizes. In Task 12, based on the number typed in R2 we have to calculate the number of the columns.

The characteristics of Task 12

- The numbers of the winners are in even columns.
- The prizes are in the odd columns.
- With the increase of the matching balls the columns decrease.
- The first column with the numbers of the winners is column 4 (D), and with the prizes is column 5 (E).

Considering all these, from the number given in R2 we have to calculate the columns.

Since every second column counts and the even and the odd columns should be separated, the number in R2 has to be multiplied by 2 (Formula 51).

$$R2\times2 \tag{51}$$

There is a negative linear proportionality between the matching numbers and columns, so there should be subtractions (Formula 52).

$$10-R2\times2 \tag{52}$$

The columns of the winners start at 4, so a translation has to be carried out (Formula 53).

$$14-R2\times2 \tag{53}$$

The algorithm of Task 12

- Pointing to the column of the numbers from cell A1.
- Pointing to the column of the prizes from cell A1.
- Calculating the sum product of the two columns.

For an easier debugging we can crop the table to five rows.

The coding of Task 12

$$\{=\text{OFFSET}(A1,1,13\text{-}R2*2,5,1)\} \tag{54}$$

$$\{=\text{OFFSET}(A1,1,14\text{-}R2*2,5,1)\} \tag{55}$$

$$\{=\text{SUM}(\text{OFFSET}(A1,1,13\text{-}R2*2,5,1)*\text{OFFSET}(A1,1,14\text{-}R2*2,5,1))\} \tag{56}$$

We can check the validity of the number given in R2.

$$\{=\text{IF}(\text{AND}(R2>=2,R2<=5),$$
$$\text{SUM}(\text{OFFSET}(A1,1,13\text{-}R2*2,5,1)*\text{OFFSET}(A1,1,14\text{-}R2*2,5,1)),$$
$$\text{"wrong number"}\} \tag{57}$$

To be sure that the number in R2 is a whole number in the [2, 5] interval, we can select it randomly (Task 13).

Task 13:	Create a random whole number in the [2, 5] interval.

This is a quite familiar task in programming. The only point in question is the interval of the random number in the programming language. This should be checked first, since the output interval of the random selection will differentiate the algorithms to a certain extent.

Both Excel and Calc create a random number in the [0, 1) interval. With geometric translations – dilation (Formula 59) and translation (Formula 61) – we can convert it into the [2, 5] interval.

The characteristics of Task 13

- It is a whole number,

49

- It is in the [2, 5] interval.

The algorithm of Task 13

- Creating a random number in the [0, 1) interval (Formula 58).
- Dilation of the interval $[0, 1) \rightarrow [0, 4)$ (Formula 59).
- Creating whole numbers $[0, 4) \rightarrow [0, 3]$ (Formula 60).
- Translation of the interval $[0, 3] \rightarrow [2, 5]$ (Formula 61).

With this algorithm there is no need for the specific built-in function, RANDBETWEEN(). Beyond that with the algorithm of creating whole random numbers in an interval students would see example of geometric transformations and practice how to handle inclusive and exclusive intervals. In addition to all of these advantages, students can be prepared for a problem quite frequent in high level programming.

The coding of Task 13

$$=\text{RAND}() \tag{58}$$

$$=\text{RAND}()*4 \tag{59}$$

$$=\text{INT}(\text{RAND}()*4) \tag{60}$$

$$=\text{INT}(\text{RAND}()*4)+2 \tag{61}$$

If we create the number of the matching balls as a random number there is no need for the validation of the number in R2. To decide on the mode of input in R2 is always the user's responsibility; both (61) with the random number and (57) with typing the number can be used.

We can select random numbers in an interval with previously unknown starting and ending values (Task 14).

Task 14: Create a random whole number in the [G2, H2] interval.

Task 14 is the generalization of Task 13.

The characteristics of Task 14

- It is a whole number.
- It is in the [G2, H2] interval.

The algorithm of Task 14

- Calculating the number of whole numbers in the [G2, H2] interval (Formula 62)
- Creating a random number in the [0, 1) interval (Formula 63).
- Dilation of the interval: $[0, 1) \rightarrow [0, H2-G2+1)$ (Formula 64).
- Creating whole numbers: $[0, H2-G2+1) \rightarrow [0, H2-G2]$ (Formula 65).
- Translation of the interval: $[0, H2-G2] \rightarrow [G2, H2]$ (Formula 66).
- Handling the "smaller-greater number" problem (Formula 67).

The coding of Task 14

=H2-G2+1	(62)
=RAND()	(63)
=RAND()*(H2-G2+1)	(64)
=INT(RAND()*(H2-G2+1))	(65)
=INT(RAND()*(H2-G2+1))+G2	(66)

Similar to Task 8, we have to handle the problem of the variables of the smaller and the greater numbers. Formula 66 should be extended with the selection of the smaller and the greater numbers, and these numbers should be used instead of the values of G2 and H2 (Formula 67).

=INT(RAND()*(MAX(G2,H2)-MIN(G2,H2)+1))+MIN(G2,H2)   (67)

www.ingramcontent.com/pod-product-compliance
Lightning Source LLC
Chambersburg PA
CBHW051215050326
40689CB00008B/1316